Introduction

Hi there!

I know how difficult it can be to get through books so I have written this book in a simple list format so that you can look for the specific skills or areas you want to focus on, pick up a few tips and use it right away. I want to stress the importance of practicing and using these tips in real life and so I encourage you to try to put these tips into practice as soon as possible to see if they are effective for you or how you can adapt them for your own purposes.

The best way to read this e-book:

There are many different ways of reading through this e-book but if you have no idea where to start, I would recommend reading through a few tips, remember those that resonated with you and then put them into practice right away. Another way to read is to go into the specific areas that you are working on, read a few tips, put down the e-book and let your brain mull over the tips and then go back to what you were working on to see if you have new ideas.

Table of Contents

CHAPTER ONE

Brainstorming speech ideas

"If at first the idea is not absurd, then there is no hope for it." - Albert Einstein

In this section, I share a few tips for helping you brainstorm ideas for speeches. If you need to create a speech from scratch but have no idea where to start, these tips will help you get started.

- **Use your own life experience** - Some of the best stories, anecdotes and situations come from your own life. Remember, whenever you make a decision, make the decision that will give you the best story afterward.
- **Talk about your work** - Have you worked on anything interesting at work lately? Were you recently promoted? The answers to these questions may give you an idea for your speech.
- **Talk about your kids** - Kids are always doing interesting things that make for fascinating stories. If you don't have a kid, try exploring something with a kid-like fascination and curiosity - you might find yourself having fun again and with an interesting idea.
- **Talk about your big purchases** - Maybe you are the kind of person that does not makes big purchases without spending a lot of time talking to people, doing your research and generally just thinking about what the big purchase means to you and your bank account. Walk others through those steps - they may find value in how you make decisions like a big purchase (especially if they are going to make similar big

purchases in the near future).

- **Explore a weird habit you have** - Everybody has weird habits. When I was younger, I always closed my closet door because I was afraid of something coming out of the closet. Weird right? Dig down deep - do you have weird habits that only a few people know? Why do you have these habits? What can other people learn about your weird habit?

- **Talk about your desires and passions** - You might have a boring life, no kids and a dead-end job but everybody that is ambitious knows where they want to be. What would you do if you couldn't fail? What would you do with unlimited money?

- **Talk about your friends (with their permission)** - If you have a variety of friends, you are almost certain to know someone that always has a story for you whenever he / she sees you. Ask them if you can share the story and then provide your perspective.

- **Read a lot** - What's the last book that you have read? Not skimmed through but really read! Why did you take the time to read through it? What was the key message of the book and why would you recommend that others read it?

- **Listen to podcasts** - Maybe you don't read - instead, why not just listen to audiobooks or podcasts while you're doing other things? I personally recommend Planet Money - short (less than 20 minutes) and sometimes quite surprising. The Dinner Party Download is another podcast that always seems to teach me something new about the world.

- **Watch t.v. / films / documentaries** - What was your favorite movie in the last year? The last 5 years? Ever? Why? What made it so good? Was it a particular actor? A scene? The world it was set in?

- **Look up random icebreaker questions for speech ideas** - If you could punch someone, who would you punch and why? If you could have any condiment come out of our belly button, which condiment would you want and why? When was the last time you did something for the first time? What was it and how did it make you feel?

CHAPTER TWO

Writing your speech

"I deal with writer's block by lowering my expectations. I think the trouble starts when you sit down to write and imagine that you will achieve something magical and magnificent—and when you don't, panic sets in. The solution is never to sit down and imagine that you will achieve something magical and magnificent. I write a little bit, almost every day, and if it results in two or three or (on a good day) four good paragraphs, I consider myself a lucky man. Never try to be the hare. All hail the tortoise." - Malcom Gladwell

My solution for writing your speech when you get writer's block: go do something productive with your time (i.e., productively procrastinate) like cleaning or exercising. When you stop thinking about what you want to write, it somehow comes to you when you're not thinking about it.

- **Outline your speech** - It always helps if you know what you need to write at the start rather than trying to piece together things as you write.
- **Leave a little bit at the end** - I can't remember where I heard this tip (and I certainly am not claiming it is an original idea) but if you are writing a speech over a number of days, leave a little bit unfinished at the end of the day so that when you pick it up again the next day, you have some momentum going for you.
- **Just write it** - Open up a blank word document (or open up a blank page in your notebook) and just write down everything that comes to your head. Maybe you already have an outline

and if so, do this for a specific section of your speech. Do not worry if it is not related to your speech - just keep writing! Once you feel like you have written down as much as you could, take a break and then come back and organize it after.

- **Constructively procrastinate** - You have to write this speech in a week you say? Feel free to procrastinate but do it productively (e.g., do the laundry, vacuum, sweep the floors). Doing mindless things may help you think more clearly (e.g., sometimes the best ideas come when you're on the toilet).

- **Tackle the easy sections first** - Don't force yourself to write something that you're blanking on. If you see another section that you have tons of ideas for, tackle that section first, build momentum and then go back to tackling the section that you were having trouble with.

- **Draw pictures** - If you feel like you just cannot bring yourself to write, try doodling or drawing a picture instead. You will probably have more fun and you might get some motivation to write from the picture you have drawn.

- **Develop an overall theme for your speech** - When I was writing essays in high school, I developed one essay that had an overall butterfly metaphor throughout my essay which outlined my 'transformation' from cocoon to butterfly in the essay. By using a theme, it can not only help your audience make a connection to something they are familiar with (and therefore, more likely to remember) but also can help you figure out the different parts of your speech and what you need to speak about in each section. For example, if you were using a butterfly example that describes your life, your beginning would talk about how you are a simple worm (i.e., your humble beginnings), the next phase would be your cocoon phase (i.e., how you prepared / trained for the next phase) and finally, your emergence as a butterfly (i.e., when you stepped out into the light and finally shined).

- **Write often and on a regular basis** - I know that when people sit down to write speeches, it often seems like a chore. It is hard writing (I know - I hate writing sometimes); however, you can change how you approach writing by writing every single day regardless of whether you want to or not. If you make it a habit (easier said than done of course), writing will be just something that you do as opposed to something you have to expend energy deciding whether or not to do.

- **Focus on the ultimate takeaway for your audience** - What is it that you want the audience to do after hearing your speech? Do you want them to take action? Do you want them to change the way they think about something that they have always thought the same way about? Do you want to sell them on your ideas? If you want the audience to takeaway something from your speech, you need a laser-like focus on that takeaway throughout your speech. If there is something in your speech that does not contribute to that takeaway message / action, you might want to rethink whether it needs to be in your speech.

CHAPTER THREE

Preparing your speech

"Give me six hours to chop down a tree and I will spend the first four sharpening the axe." - Abraham Lincoln

After writing a speech, what can you do to best prepare for the speech? Here are a few of the things that I have seen that help speakers prepare for their speech.

- **Practice your speech in chunks** - Practicing in chunks will help prevent memory lapses where you have previously practiced the whole speech at once. If you practice in chunks, it also helps you readjust the speech easier than if you had memorized the speech as a whole.
- **Memorize big ideas, don't memorize speeches word for word** - This is similar to the tip above and helps to both prevent memory lapses during your speech and mitigating the lapses if they do occur during your speech. Memorizing word for word means that speakers will be delivering their speech word for word and if they miss a word and then stumble, they will need the exact words to get back on track. If you memorize big ideas and practice delivering those ideas in your own words, you are more likely to know your speech better and be able to recover from any stumbles. This will also allow you to adjust your speech as appropriate (news headlines occurring that day, hearing stories from other speakers or the audience, etc.)
- **Write down quotes and other statements you need the exact words for in your speech on mini flash cards** - There are times where you do need to know things word for word (e.g.,

quotes, statements, statistics, figures). I like to either memorize these until I know them by heart or I write them down on flash cards (in large letters) and then refer to them as appropriate during the speech. I try not to make it obvious that I am referring to the cards so depending on what I want to refer to, I will say "I want to get the exact wording right because this quote / statistic / statement is important". I will then refer to my flash card and deliver it. This is also a great way to review your notes / material in case you completely forget what's next in your speech.

- **Prepare an introduction that introduces you as a speaker** - A typical introduction contains the the speaker's experience and credentials and why the speaker is the best person to speak on the subject, why the speech is relevant to the audience at this time, the speech title and then finally the speaker's name. The introduction serves as a way of bridging the gap between the speaker, who may be a complete stranger and the audience, who needs to understand why they are spending their time listening to this speaker.

- **Think about your audience** - Ask yourself who your audience is. How old are they? What are they interested in? What kind of t.v. shows and films do they watch? What are the key messages and actions that you want them to take away? What kind of objections will they have and how can you address those objections?

- **Try to understand what environment you will be speaking in before you give your speech** - Will there be a lectern? Microphone and speakers? A stage? Spotlights? Understanding your environment will help you understand what you need as a speaker and what you might need to adapt to the environment in order to deliver the best speech possible.

- **If you have props, make sure you have a backup plan** - This is only important if you use props in your speech but you should always have a backup plan in case your props do not work OR you somehow forget to bring your props for the speech. This applies to PowerPoint presentations as well (technology seems to have a knack at failing during critical moments on stage). If you are presenting a presentation on your computer, make sure that you are ready to speak even if your laptop does not work. If you have pictures that you want to pass out to the audience, make sure you have multiple copies for everyone (in fact, extra copies can never be a bad thing).

- **Time yourself as you practice** - I have been an audience member for speeches that ran way overtime and I can tell you that audience members think about anything but the speech when speakers go way past their allotted time. Time yourself when you are practicing and give yourself a small buffer of time so that you can improvise and adjust your speech as needed for disruptions. Ideally, your speech shouldn't be too short (e.g., 5 minute speech for a 30 minute time slot) but it shouldn't be too long either so I would aim for a 25 -27 minute speech with a 30 minute time slot to provide time for introductions, applause, laughter and pauses.

- **Practice it live in front of an audience if you can** - Your audience could be a family member, a spouse, a partner or it could even be a pet. It helps if you can deliver your speech in an environment as similar as possible to the real event to prepare yourself as best as you can.

CHAPTER FOUR

Speech do's and don'ts

"Mistakes are always forgivable, if one has the courage to admit them." - Bruce Lee

After doing over 50 speeches, evaluating over 100 speeches and judging various speech contests, there are a number of speech do's and don'ts that you should be aware of and I share them here:

Speech do's
- **Be social** - Try to talk to other people before your speech, especially people that you might be delivering your speech to. This can help you calm your nerves and it can be quite a confidence boost to see someone in the crowd that you are familiar with. People want you to succeed (and this is especially the case if they have gotten to know you).
- **Talk to the organizer of the event** - It can be a nice way to break the ice and to learn about issues that previous speakers have faced and what the organizer (or you) can do to address them (e.g., a loud air conditioner in the back).
- **Make sure that any visuals you present can be seen by all audience members** - If any visuals cannot be seen by audience members, you might be able to describe the picture but I recommend that you either use visuals that are large enough to be seen by everyone (even those at the very back of the venue) or do not use visuals at all.
- **Ask the organizer for a glass of water** - This isn't needed for all speeches but for especially long speeches, a glass of water can go a long way in parching your throat and giving you a

much needed break (imagine talking for hours - I can't imagine doing it without small breaks in between!)

- **Dress appropriately** - If you are not sure of how you should dress for your speech, dress more formally than you think you need to and dress down if appropriate. You can always dress down but you can't always dress more formally if the occasion necessitates it. Depending on the event, it might be more appropriate to dress down to the level of the audience (to signify that you're not different from them) or to dress one level above the audience (e.g., suit if the audience is mostly wearing jeans) to project professionalism.

- **Walk confidently up to the stage** - Everything leading up to your speech (your speech introduction, how you walk up, whether you are smiling as you walk up) helps give the audience the impression that everything will be a success and that they will get a lot out of the speech. Not doing these things may make the audience question you even before you deliver your speech!

Speech dont's

- **Don't chew gum while speaking** - Yes, I have seen people chew gum while speaking and this is as awful as it sounds. Not only does it look weird but more importantly, it can distort your speech. Even worse, you may spit it out mid-sentence and that is just not something you want to recover from during a speech.

- **Don't pace nervously or shift your weight from side to side** - When people are nervous, it seems to calm them down when they can walk around; however, if you walk around too much, it shows that you are nervous and / or restless and neither are good for portraying confidence in your speech.

- **Don't hold a click pen in your hand while speaking** - Oh god, the clicks! I did this for my first speech because I thought it would help facilitate great hand gestures but I was so nervous that I was clicking the pen throughout the whole speech and I didn't even notice it until someone pointed it out after the speech. Do you want the audience counting how many times you click your pen or do you want the audience to be listening to your speech?

- **Don't eat anything strange before your speech** - There are butterflies in your stomach, you are nervous about your speech - why eat that strange sushi from the gas station to compound all this? Eat a light meal that you normally eat and make nausea and food poisoning one less thing to worry about during your speech.

CHAPTER FIVE

Your speech introduction

"In making a speech one must study three points: first, the means of producing persuasion; second, the language; third the proper arrangement of the various parts of the speech." - Aristotle

The first part of the speech (the speech introduction) is more important than some people realize. Speech introductions can enthrall people and tease them for what's to come; don't let that opportunity slip away with a boring speech introduction!

- **Start with a quote, rhetorical question or a surprising fact** - I got this tip from a speaker that has been in the business for over 40 years - he has found that the three most effective ways of starting a speech are with a quote (something that is particularly relevant to your speech and by someone that is generally well-known works well), a rhetorical question (a question that makes the audience think something but does not give them an opportunity to answer) and a surprising fact (did you know that 1 in 3 people think that fractions are imaginary). Each of these ways gives you something to 'hook' the audience and draw them into your speech.
- **Address the audience** - This tip works well if you know a few people in the audience before you deliver a speech. You look like an incredibly well-polished speaker if you can address specific audience members by name throughout your speech.
- **Provide background and context on your speech subject** - Think about the audience that you are delivering this speech to - are they well-educated? Do they know anything about the subject that you are talking about? Try not to assume anything

about your audience. If you provide the audience enough background so that they can understand what you will be talking about, you can establish a baseline of knowledge for the audience on which to build upon.

- **Provide a thesis statement that states exactly what you hope to accomplish in this speech** - Try to listen to a t.v. show or a movie in a random place for 7 minutes - it won't be easy to understand what's going on without some context. The thesis statement in your speech outlines exactly what you will tell the audience and therefore, is a great way of showing the audience that you want to make it as easy as possible for them to follow and understand the message you are delivering.

- **Use teasers in your introduction** - If you do not want to provide an outline of your speech, you can use teasers so that the audience members have a faint idea on what you are going to share but not the full idea until you get to it.

- **Do something that captures the audience's attention (e.g., sing, yell, or use prolonged silence)** - Most people, when they listen to speeches, aren't expecting people to sing or yell. If you find that your audience is not paying attention (for example, if you are making a speech while people are eating), then try to do something that can get the audience's attention by showcasing the unexpected.

- **Keep it short** - Most speeches will have a time limit - try not to use all of your time in the speech introduction. Try to keep it short so that you can get to the main body of your speech.

- **Try to incorporate your speech title (e.g., as part of your thesis statement)** - The speech title is the first thing that the audience learns about your speech and by using your speech title throughout your speech, you help reinforce your overall message with your audience.

- **Only include what is sufficient and necessary for your speech in the introduction** - For some speakers, I have noticed an exhaustive background story or an explanation of the context before the speech and this, in my opinion, can be better served by using the speaker introduction to explain this. Some background is certainly necessary but try to use the speaker introduction (i.e., the introduction to introduce you) as effectively as possible so that you can make your speech concise and focused.

Wang Yip

CHAPTER SIX

Your speech body

"Eloquent speech is not from lip to ear, but rather from heart to heart."
- William Jennings Bryan

The speech body is where your main facts, opinions or arguments are presented. The tips below will help you make your speech more memorable and interesting.

- **Incorporate different figurative language** - Use figurative language like metaphors, similes, hyperboles, etc. to help paint a vivid picture for your audience. These can also be used to help introduce some humour into your speech.
- **Use simple metaphors** - When I say simple metaphors, I mean using a comparison that the audience is familiar with. For example, if you are trying to explain how the brain works, you can talk about how the brain is very similar to a library (e.g., it stores information, there is a catalog system similar to how the brain organizes information, etc.) People might not know anything about the brain but they understand how a library works and can map something complex to something they understand.
- **Structure your speech in a logical way** - Think about what you are trying to show through your speech. Are you trying to show a trend? Structure your speech chronologically. Are you trying to make an argument? Present the positives and negatives of both sides of the argument.
- **Use transitions between different points** - Any little thing that can help the audience follow your speech means a more effective speech. "From the telegraph, we moved to the

telephone which is the second point along my road map to the internet."

- **Pause to signify the end / beginning of a point** - A pause helps the audience think about what you just said and provide a natural end to a point in your speech.

- **Try not to cover more than three main points** - This isn't a hard and fast rule but the audience has a better chance of remembering your speech if you cover three points. The three points is a natural number for your speech but it may vary depending on the length and subject of your speech.

- **Repeat as needed to increase understanding and retention** - Don't be afraid to repeat certain points that you feel you want to ingrain in your audience's minds. "Practice productive procrastination. Let me say that again because I think this is really important. Practice productive procrastination."

- **Think about how the speech body fits in terms of timing for the overall speech** - If you think about an essay, the introduction is slightly bigger than the conclusion but the bulk of the essay is in its body. A speech is structured in a similar fashion - the speech body represents the bulk of the speech and therefore, there should be enough content / arguments / facts to support the majority of your speech time.

- **Ask rhetorical questions to highlight key points** - Rhetorical questions can be a great device in helping direct the audience to specific things you want them to think about. I have seen rhetorical questions used as a way of priming the audience with specific thoughts (I will give you a second to think about what you would do with a million dollars), adding suspense to stories (What was the man doing in the alley?), or to point out how ridiculous something appears to be (Why in the world would I jump out of a plane without a parachute?).

CHAPTER SEVEN

Speak with your body

"Body language is a very powerful tool. We had body language before we had speech, and apparently, 80% of what you understand in a conversation is read through the body, not the words." - Deborah Bull

The statistics all say different numbers but it is impossible to deny the fact that body language is an important part of communication. What is your body language communicating and is it congruent to what you are saying? It is weird to see someone smiling while talking about their pet passing away on the weekend - make sure that your body language matches the words coming out of your mouth.

- **Hold your arms at your sides until you need to use them** - Many people have natural body language and arm gestures that they subconsciously use while they speak. If you don't naturally speak with your hands (notice the next time you speak with friends or family) then leave them by the side. Hand gestures is great for emphasizing parts of your speech but too many hand gestures can dilute the hand gestures that you do use.
- **Pick three different places on the stage to walk between** - I have noticed that some speakers have found it a challenge to use the whole speaking space. Choose three different places on the stage to walk between and spend a few paragraphs (or about 5 - 10 sentences) in each spot. For example, if there are three spots (left, middle right), start in the middle for your introduction, move to the right (or left) for the first point in your speech, then the middle for your second point and then

to the left (or right) for the third and last point of your speech. Finally, to end your speech, come to the middle again. You won't be walking around too much and you will have effectively used the speaking space given to you.

- **Do not fidget with pens, your arms or your clothing** - Fidgeting, of any sort, shows that you are nervous and does not give a good impression to the audience that the speaker is confident. If you find that you are fidgeting, try practicing your speech in front of the mirror and noticing what happens when you get nervous. If you fidget with your hands, try holding your wrist in front of you or behind you. If you fidget and shift your body weight from side to side, try focusing on one spot. Ultimately, you will gain confidence as you do more speeches.

- **Have good posture** - In addition to making you appear like a confident speaker, standing up straight will also give your lungs more capacity to take in air and give you more time to speak before needing to take a breath.

- **Hold your head up high as you speak** - Holding your head up high will help your posture and again, give the appearance of a confidence speaker. Think about the last time you spoke to someone who had their head down low - what did you think? Were they lying? Hiding something? Not happy? What will the audience think if your head is held down low?

- **Say 'cheese'** - Smile as you come out and smile throughout your speech (if appropriate). Smiling helps give you confidence and it helps to relax the audience (and your nerves) as you deliver your speech.

- **Practice the power pose (the victory "V") to gain confidence** - The power pose works! Check out Amy Cuddy's Ted Talk on the power pose and what it can do to your confidence. This isn't something to do as part of your speech but it is a great way to gain some confidence before your speech.

- **If you still feel like you have no confidence, fake it** - Like everyone says, you should fake it until you make it. No one can tell if you are faking confidence or if you are actually confident; the trick is faking it long enough until you are confident.

- **Try to use your hands to emphasize different messages** - Your hand gestures can be used to emphasize different parts of your speech. For example, you can use your hands to place events in chronological order. You can use your hands to form certain shapes that might be relevant to your speech. You can use your hands to emphasize different facial gestures (like surprise, shock or hunger) as part of a story. Do not be afraid to experiment but also use any exaggerated emphasis sparingly.

- **Do not be afraid to 'act' out a scene if it helps your speech** - Again, this goes back to how hand gestures and body language can help emphasize different parts of your speech. For example, I did a speech about visiting the Great Wall of China and I physically showed my audience how I literally sometimes climbed the stairs up the wall due to the uneven blocks. The audience may be able to get a sense of how big the wall is through words alone but showing them by acting it out can help paint an even clearer picture for the audience.

- **Try to go as close to the audience as you are comfortable with** - Although it can depend on your speech and speech content, getting close to the audience can provide a more engaging and intimate ambiance as a speaker and it can seem as if you are really talking to them specifically rather than the audience as a whole. I don't do this very often as it can make certain audience members uncomfortable but I like to do this sparingly to make certain points (like pointing out exemplary audience members).

CHAPTER EIGHT

Improving your vocal variety

"People often ask me how I developed my vocal sound, and the answer usually disappoints them: 'It's just the way I sound when I sing.'" - Michael Franks

Your voice is the medium through which your audience will understand you. Although a lot of communication is non-verbal, your audience won't be able to fully understand you if you don't use your voice so it is an important part of speaking. If you're having a hard time trying to figure out how to add vocal variety to your speech, imagine that you are telling your story to kids. They will react to loud noises, be sensitive to softer voices and get a sense of how exciting your speech is through the pace and rate at which you speak.

- **Find your rhythm** - Everybody speaks with a certain tone, pace and volume; if you know what your normal speaking voice is like then you will be able to identify the different ways you can change it through pace, tone and volume.
- **Speed up to add suspense or enthusiasm to your speech** - Talking at the same rhythm can make you monotonous as a speaker. Notice how storytellers increase the rhythm of their speech during exciting or suspenseful parts of their stories. The same technique can be applied to your speeches, even if you aren't telling a story and that rhythm can help create suspense or excitement for things that aren't normally suspenseful or exciting.
- **Slow down when you are describing something important to the audience** - On the other hand, slowing down can signal to

the audience something that is extremely important or something that should be taken seriously. You can also use rhythm to add humour to your speech as well, especially when you want to deliver a punch line that might not be obvious to the audience. I generally slow down my speaking and use pauses to help emphasize important parts of my speech (e.g., (normal rate of speaking) There are three things that are important to any speech: (slower rate of speaking) 1 (pause) organization, 2 (pause) understanding the speech's purpose and 3 (pause) a call to action.)

- **Talk in a booming voice to grab the audience's attention** - Depending on the situation, you may want to try a scream or a yell during your speech to really grab the audience's attention or to really make a punchline more effective. Very few speakers yell and you can use this in combination with a whisper (the next tip) to really add contrast to different points in your speech or to just be different. Use this sparingly because yelling isn't the most effective way of communicating things to an audience and does not make a connection or have that intimate feel that a normal conversational voice has.

- **Talk in a slight whisper when you are talking about something serious or to add contrast** - Using this in conjunction with loud sounds can help to add a very effective contrast to different points in your speech. For instance, if you are telling a story, you can use your louder voice to express anger and then a slightly softer voice than normal to denote a calmer presence.

- **Make sure that your normal volume can be heard by all listeners** - One of the worst things that can happen to a speaker is not being heard and although some speakers handle this well, I've never been good with interruptions by audience members asking me to speak louder. Don't risk this happening to you - test your volume beforehand or at the beginning of your speech to ensure that everyone can hear you.

CHAPTER NINE

Adding humour

"From there to here, and here to there, funny things are everywhere." - Dr. Seuss

Conclude your speech with a bang! Let the audience know the most important details of your speech in the conclusion and end on a strong note.

- **Explore the different tools of humour (i.e., the tools of the English language):**
  - **Sarcasm** - Sarcasm is an expression or statement that means the complete opposite of what the person who said it meant. For example, I heard a speech about a man who went to a restaurant and tried authentic Mexican food that was incredibly hot and spicy just to prove to his female friends that he was man enough to eat authentic food. As it so happened, he was burned at the end of his story, both literally and metaphorically but a nice sarcastic phrase at the end could be a whimpering voice where he says "I was definitely man enough for the authentic spicy Mexican food".
  - **Irony** - Irony is a statement that shows that there is a difference between what was said and what happened in reality. For example, I have previously talked about how humble I am as a person and then saying how awesome I am with my next statement. I personally find that irony works best when the different statements (the appearance of things and the reality) are close together in the speech or if it is extremely

obvious, based on the theme of your speech

- **Hyperbole** - Hyperboles are exaggerated statements or claims that are meant to emphasize something but not meant to be taken literally. 'The man was so fat, there were planets orbiting around him.' Or 'My friend was so dumb that he tripped over a wireless telephone'. Hyperboles can be a nice way of adding additional humour to irony.
- **Similes / Metaphors** - Similes and metaphors are where you compare one thing to another. "Speeches should be like a skirt, short enough to keep it interesting but long enough to cover the essentials". As you can see, it can be a great way of helping people understand a difficult concept but it can also be a way of surprising the audience with something humorous. It can be difficult to find something that works but you can always look up humorous similes and metaphors online that you might be able to use (or go for the complete opposite - e.g., the ship flew in the air not like a falling brick" - a trick that was used by Douglas Adams)

- **Impressions** - I found a good way to add humour to your speech is to do an impression even if its only passable. If you can use quotes from that person and the quotes are directly relevant to your speech, it will be that much funnier. Practice (or learn) through watching youtube videos. Kevin Spacey is an excellent celebrity to learn impressions from though my only advice is to make sure that the impressions are modern enough so that your audience can understand it right away without your explanation.
- **Rhyming** - I have used this as a way of introducing rhythm and suspense to my speech - when I delivered one of my speeches with rhymes, an audience member said that he had to remember to stop laughing so hard so that he could keep up with the rhymes and it can make your speech even better. Of course, with rhyming, this means that you have to know your whole speech word for word but it might be worth it to have that extra humour in your speech. (E.g., I talked about the birds and the bees and Korea; I was eloquent without pauses; my speech flowed like diarrhea). The way I come up with

rhymes is to figure out my rhyming scheme and then what words I want to rhyme; I then come up with sentences to 'fit' the words into.

- **Ask questions** - For some jokes, a punchline phrased in a question could be a better way of delivering it then in a statement. I like using questions as a way of getting the audience to think and to come up with their own punchline. Using questions can also be an effective way of 'priming' the audience with specific facts or a line of thinking that they may not have been thinking about.

- **Create inside jokes with the audience** - The most effective speakers seem to have a knack for relating back to things that the audience members know. It might have been a previous joke or a speech tip that the audience members recently heard from a previous speaker at the same event or it could even be a recent news headline or piece. This helps to create a special 'inside' joke of sorts and gives the speaker a special connection with the audience.

- **Explore the timing of your pauses before punchlines** - It might seem like a long time but giving the audience a few seconds before delivering a punchline can be an effective way of making the audience laugh, especially with jokes with long stories or complicated setups.

- **Build on your jokes** - It can be a huge challenge to come up with joke after joke in your speech. Build on your existing jokes and try to 'milk' it as much as you can. A lot of stand up comedians do this in a very funny way and you can do this in your speech to get a few extra laughs without having to come up with brand new jokes throughout your speech

- **Make fun of yourself** - Using self-deprecating humour can be a fantastic way of connecting to the audience because it can show that you are not serious about yourself and that you can take a joke. The best thing about self-deprecating humour is that there is a small chance that you might offend someone (whereas there may be a bigger chance with jokes that get a laugh at the expense of an audience member).

CHAPTER TEN

Be intentional with your language

"Choose your words and actions wisely. They can be forgiven, but not forgotten." - Isaiah Harden

Words can have a tremendous impact on the audience. A concept that I learned a long time ago during my leadership experiences in University is the idea of 'framing' or 'reframing'. It is otherwise known as spin and using the appropriate words can put a positive or negative spin on a situation (and thus the overall ambiance or situation). My university was going through quite a bit of construction (and people joked that it was actually a season at the university) and while one of my coworkers was giving a tour to visitors, one of the visitors said that there seemed to be a lot of construction and she said "the university is constantly improving its facilities and services for students". It was a clever way of framing the construction as a positive for the university and its students and speaks to the power of the words that you choose in your speech.

- **Consider your audience** - The audience can be a key factor in determining the types of words you use. Are you using complex words with a lot of acronyms and abbreviations? You may have to explain these in your speech with certain audiences (and you might have to do that anyway just to be safe).
- **Choose simple words** - As much as possible, you want to use simple words that your audience has no trouble understanding. Always strive for the simplest word possible (e.g., instead of complication, use problem; instead of

comprehend, use understand). Your audience will not be impressed by million dollar words but they will be impressed by simple words with profound messages and actions.

- **Understand that the language that you use can have an effect on your audience** - Imagine that you are trying to describe your recent vacation to Europe. You describe with vivid words how you laid on the beach and embraced the warm sun, how you ate juicy olives that just burst in your mouth when you bit into it, and how you breathed in the fresh air from the ocean. The audience gets a very different picture if all you said was that you laid on the beach, ate olives and breathed in fresh air. It all depends on what kind of image you want the audience to picture. I recently witnessed a speech that talked about how a man was very down in his life and then turned things around and the language that the speaker used helped to portray how down and depressing his life was before his turning point and then he used very positive language to paint the new reality after his turning point. Language can even help turn negatives into opportunities (e.g., he takes a long time to work -> he is detail oriented)

- **Repetition can be an effective tool** - Sometimes even if you slow down your pace of speech and use simple language, the audience may not retain the message. Repeat key messages throughout your speech and tell your audience what you want them to take away.

- **Minimize your crutch words** - If you are using crutch words, it does not mean that you are not a good speaker but having no crutch words, awkward phrases, long silences shows that you have put in the time to put that extra polish on your speech. Think of it as a nice cherry on top of the already decadent cheesecake that is your speech - it adds that ineffably extra thing about your speech although it is not required. If you have lots of crutch words (think about how many times you say um, ah, etc. The next time you speak), you can eliminate them through the same strategy that I used and that is to not say any crutch words at all any time you interact with anyone. It requires concentration and focus but over time, your crutch words will go away as you force yourself to speak cleanly.

CHAPTER ELEVEN

Purposeful eye contact

"Sometimes you have to disconnect to stay connected. Remember the old days when you had eye contact during a conversation? When everyone wasn't looking down at a device in their hands? We've become so focused on that tiny screen that we forget the big picture, the people right in front of us." - Regina Brett

If the audience is looking at you, how are you connecting with them? Eye contact shows that you notice them in the audience and has a personal touch. Go to the coffee shop and sit there watching couples - can you tell what kind of relationship they have through their eye contact?

- **Try to look (really look) into people's eyes as you speak** - If you find that looking into people's eyes is too uncomfortable for you as you are speaking then try looking at the top of their heads or their mouths (tip: audiences won't be able to tell that you're not looking directly into their eyes).
- **Try not to look everywhere at once** - It looks unnatural and very strange and it is not the best way to make a connection with your audience, instead…
- **Pick and choose 5 people to look at in the audience** - For large audiences, pick and choose 5 different people to look at and then cycle through the same people on a regular basis (you might be more comfortable choosing people you're familiar with). This gives the appearance that you are speaking to everyone in the audience and can be a more effective way of connecting to the audience than trying to look at everyone.

- **Hold and maintain eye contact** - If you talk to someone who only looks at you for a second here and there every minute, you would not feel very 'connected' with them. Therefore, as a speaker, it is important to hold and maintain eye contact for at least a sentence or two in order to really connect with them and then move on to the next audience member.
- **Try not to look down or look up** - This is something that I seem to do whenever I am thinking about what to say next. It is hard to do but try to maintain eye contact with your audience while thinking of the next part of your speech.

CHAPTER TWELVE

End with a bang - your speech conclusion

"Lord Chancellor, did I deliver the speech well? I am glad of that, for there was nothing in it." - George III

Conclude your speech with a bang! Let the audience know the most important details of your speech in the conclusion and end on a strong note. If you want the audience to takeaway a key message or action, the speech's conclusion is the place to tell the audience.

- **Review the points that you have covered in your speech (but don't repeat)** - There are two ways to recap the main points in your speech: you can repeat the main points or you can 'add on' to the main points in your speech. As an example, if your speech was about being more productive and your three points were: try to spend 'off' time productively, try to multi-task safe activities and set deadlines then you might conclude your speech by suggesting example ideas for each of the main points in your speech. A sample conclusion might be: "Today, I talked about being more productive through doing things like using 5 or 10 minutes of wait time during the day productively by reading a news article or drawing, doing the laundry and cleaning while the laundry is running and doing some sweeping or cleaning the dishes just before you have to head out with friends".

- **End with an action that everyone can do** - A speech is much stronger when you can provide an action that everyone can do in 5 minutes that can immediately improve their lives. If your speech is about confidence, talk about how doing the "V" pose can help increase your confidence (Watch Amy Cuddy's Ted Talk on youtube). It's easy to do and everyone can do it after your speech.

- **End with a story that captures the key message you want to pass on to your audience** - If you can't end with an action, leave your audience with a story that they can share with others. For centuries, information was passed down from generation to generation through stories and I believe we still remember things better when it is presented in a story than when it is presented in straight facts. You probably know of a fairy tale that you heard about when you were young but can't remember a particular subject that you learned more recently in university or high school.

- **Try to incorporate your speech title (e.g., to end your speech)** - Again with the speech title! It's a great way of solidifying your speech with the audience and since it is the first and last thing that the audience hears, this can be a nice way of sandwiching your speech in a structured way.

- **If ending on a humourous note, end with your punchline to leave them laughing and applauding** - A great humourous story at the end of your speech can be a great way to end on a positive note. There is also a greater chance that the audience will remember the punchline (and the story) so tying in your key takeaway into the punchline can be an effective tool for reinforcing the message in the audience's minds.

CHAPTER THIRTEEN

After the speech - feedback

"For good ideas and true innovation, you need human interaction, conflict, argument, debate." - Margaret Heffernan

Chances are good that after you speak, many people will comment on what they thought about the speech or how it might have impacted them. This is a fantastic opportunity for you to gain invaluable feedback on your own speech (and how to improve it for next time) as well as gain ideas for future speeches that you can give.

- **Take note of the parts of your speech that audience members liked or disliked** - Although one or two members should not be taken as a barometer for success or failure, you should note down different patterns or trends in what listeners thought. I think if 3 - 5 listeners have commented on something in particular, I would note it down and make sure that I take a look at it later to see what I can learn / what I can improve upon.
- **If they have a few minutes, ask them how they might improve things** - If listeners did not like specific parts of your speech, make sure you ask them why and how it can be improved, if appropriate. I think a lot of listeners would normally be intimidated by professional speakers so I myself, for instance, would not approach or give feedback to professional speakers but I do not consider myself a professional speaker (yet) and seek feedback when possible.
- **Note down specific language that they use that you might be able to use in your speech** - Listening to people speak about

how your speech has impacted them can be a great opportunity to listen to the specific language that they use and to gain deeper insight into how they think and what you need to do to convince them of your key message, action or takeaway.

- **Explore ideas for future speeches** - Often times, if you speak about X, audience members will ask you about X but they may also ask you about Y and Z as well. You may have the answers to their questions but think about why they are asking these questions and try to see if there are opportunities for future speeches that address those concerns.
- **Remember that it is not personal** - Try not to be discouraged if you receive criticisms on your speech or your delivery. No speech is perfect and there are always opportunities to improve so take every speech as a step towards a perfect speech.

Want more?

I NEED MORE WANG!!!

Previously, I wrote about the different elements of public speaking based on my experience in Toastmasters. I have five books on the topic of public speaking and all of these books can be found on Amazon (search for 'Amazon Wang Yip' to find my author page and links to all of my books).

Public Speaking

- 50 awesome ideas for table topics: Challenge members, attract guests and have fantastic meetings
- Make your speech more impactful: Top 10 tips (+ 1 bonus tip) on making and delivering a great speech
- A Guide to Evaluating Speeches: How to prepare, construct and provide impactful evaluations
- How to create and deliver great speeches: A seven day approach

Habits

- Essential Habits: Actions, strategies and directives to take your life to the next level

Courses

I have three courses on Udemy that might interest you:

* * *

- Tips on the first 10 basic speaking skills everyone needs - a course that covers the first 10 skills to be an effective public speaker. I cover what those skills are and some of my personal experience in working on those skills and what I do in my speeches.
- Make your speech more impactful - based on my best selling book - this is a course that demonstrates the specific strategies and tactics that I use to make a speech from "oh yeah somebody did a speech" to "Oh wow, that speech was amazing". Based on my 10+ years of experience, these are the things that I see the best speakers do and I break it down into specific things that you can mimic and incorporate into your presentations.
- So you want to become a management consultant.... A course developed by myself and a former colleague at Deloitte based on our experience going through the interview process both as an interviewee and as an interviewer. We cover how to network your way into a management consulting job, interview prep, case study strategies and more tips to help you get that job in management consulting.

Blog

I am an avid writer and I blog at steemit.com/wcy, on medium (@wangyip) and on my personal site (wangyip.ca). If you are interested in more, I also provide a summary of the books I read every month in my newsletter and you can sign up at wangyip.ca.

www.ingramcontent.com/pod-product-compliance
Lightning Source LLC
Chambersburg PA
CBHW070930220526
45468CB00005B/1727